The
TOTE
BAG

LAURENCE KING

Published in 2011 by
Laurence King Publishing Ltd
361–373 City Road
London EC1V 1LR
United Kingdom
Tel: + 44 20 7841 6900
Fax: + 44 20 7841 6910
e-mail: enquiries@laurenceking.com
www.laurenceking.com

A catalogue record for this book is
available from the British Library

ISBN: 978-1-85669-730-9

Book Design: Jai Studio
www.jaistudio.co.uk
Printed in China

Commissioning editor:
Helen Rochester
Tote bag/cover illustration © 2011
Gemma Correll
www.gemmacorrell.com

Jitesh Patel has several years'
experience in illustration and design,
and set up his multi-disciplinary
studio, Jai Studio, in Shoreditch,
London, in 2007. His clients include
British Airways, Christie's the
auctioneers, Duck and Cover clothing,
The Economist, French Connection,
Galaxy chocolate, *The Guardian*,
Publicis & Hal Riney San Francisco,
HSBC, Jack Wills, John Lewis, John
Murray Publishing, Jury & Co, MTV,
Ted Baker, Tesco, TBWA, Tres
Generaciones and Vodafone.

In January 2009, Jitesh Patel
launched the Tote Prints blog
(toteprints.wordpress.com) to
celebrate his large collection of tote
bags. The idea is to create a platform
to bring together artists and tote bag
prints and to showcase them to a
wider audience.

Jitesh Patel's work has been featured
in numerous magazines, newspapers
and books, including the book *300%
Cotton* by Helen Walters (Laurence
King Publishing), *IdN Magazine* and
Computer Arts magazine.

www.jiteshpatel.co.uk

The TOTE BAG

JITESH *Patel*

Laurence King Publishing

Contents

006	**Introduction**
008	Aaron D. Carámbula
009	Adam Augustyn
010	Alícia Roselló & Elisa Riera
011	Andre Weier
012	Andrea Forgacs
013	Andy Ainger
014	Andrew Bannecker
016	Angie McCarthy
017	Anke Weckmann
018	Angus Hyland
020	Ashkahn
021	Ashley Jessiman
022	Bart Aalbers
024	Becky Redman
025	Bosque Studio
026	Bratislav Milenkovic
027	Carla & Hugo
028	Caroline Roach
029	Catalina Estrada for Purocorazón
030	Central Illustration Agency
031	Chris Judge
032	Chris Piascik
033	Colm Larkin
034	Christopher & Kathleen Sleboda
038	Claudia Brown & Jessie Whipple Vickery
040	Dave Hughes
041	David Denosowicz & Maggie Doyle
042	Dom Murphy
043	eBoy
044	Elena Gallen

045	Erika Firm
046	Fabian Monheim
047	Fita Frattini Caica
048	Gabe Wong
049	Gabrijela Bulatovic
050	Gemma Busquets
051	Gemma Correll
052	Gemma Latimer
053	Gemma Shiel
054	GraphicAirlines
056	Hanna Melin
057	Hannah Goudge
058	Hannah Chipkin
060	Hannah Stouffer
061	Hen Weekend
062	Hideo Kawamura
063	HUGE
064	Ian Stevenson
065	Ingrid Reithaug & Tonje Holand
066	Jason Ponggasam & Patty Variboa
067	Jason Scuderi
068	Jeremyville
070	Jitesh Patel
071	Joe Rogers
072	John McFaul, Ollie Munden & Chris Malbon
074	John Derian
075	Jon Burgerman
076	Jon Knox
077	Jon Simmons
078	Josephine Ada Chinonye Chime
079	Josh Cochran
080	Julia Nielsen

081	Julia Pott
082	Julie Courtois
083	Kai Clements & Anthony Sunter
084	Kalene Rivers & Dan Weise
088	Karin Söderquist
089	Karl Grandin & Björn Atldax
090	Karo Akpokiere
091	Kaza Razat & Imani Powell
092	Kazuko Nomoto
093	Kittozutto
094	Kyle Stewart
096	Lucie Sheridan
098	Little Factory
099	Make Art Your Zoo
100	Manja Radic
101	Mar Hernández
102	Marcia Copeland
103	Maria Holmer Dahlgren
104	Martynas Birskys
105	Mary Gaynor
106	Mas Shafreen
107	Megan Price
108	Medicom
110	Mel Lim
111	Miguel Melgarejo
112	Morris Lee
114	Nadja Girod
115	Nina Palmer
116	Noëla Parant
117	Paul Farrell
118	Pepa Prieto
120	Pianofuzz
121	Proud Creative
122	Progress Packaging
126	Rachel Gannon
127	Rachel Rheingold & Michael Berick
128	Rob Marshbank
130	Ros Shiers
131	Russell Reid
132	Rupert Meats
134	Sara Hoover
135	Sara Jensen
136	Sarah J. Coleman
138	Sarah Wilkins
139	Sarajo Frieden
140	Shinzi Katoh
142	Sonia Brit
143	Stefan Tijs
144	Stewart Walker
145	Suzie Brown
146	Tatiana Arocha
147	Tofu Girls
148	Tommy Higson
149	Toormix
150	Ulla Puggaard
151	Valerie Thai
152	Valistika Studio
153	Vicky Newman
154	Yi Yu Shen
155	Zaihasriah Zahidi
156	Zeke Wade
157	Zena McKeown & Ben Roberts
158	Zeptonn
159	Zosen
160	**Thanks**

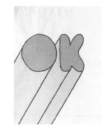

Introduction

The tote bag is an eco product for this century, destined to replace disposable plastic bags. The canvas bag has become increasingly popular in recent years, as more people have become environmentally conscious, concerned about climate change and aware of the impact of their carbon footprint. The media reminds us all to be more conscious of the world we live in, and environmental issues are inescapable.

I have been a collector of tote bags since they first started to emerge a few years ago. I am drawn to the unique, beautiful and original designs and illustrations that feature on many of them. It was this love that prompted me to start a blog about tote bags and the designers who create them. The blog attracted many visitors interested in the designs and their creators. The next step for me, naturally, was to write a book about tote bags, plotting the journey of totes from their functional roots to their manifestation today as a fashion statement.

The tote bag artworks that are most striking, inventive, ironic and original have formed the basis of this book. I have received many positive and encouraging responses from designers while researching the topic; most have commented that it was a great subject for a book. I hope the readers of this book will share our enthusiasm.

Many of the designers that I interviewed mentioned the fact that people are steadily moving away from using disposable plastic bags and more towards using reusable commodities, as part of a growing trend to reuse and recycle materials. The tote bag, as well as having eco credentials, is also a great artistic opportunity; it offers an amazing blank canvas on which anything can be created, and it is very affordable. Tote bags address our cultural and social needs, and tote bag designers look for fresh, young-minded people to wear them and help them become 'environmental action detonators' – or at least a 'placebo for people's ecological conscience'.

Tote bags have also begun to emerge as an extension of clothing and style. The printed design on a tote bag can be used as a message to communicate someone's personality and display their individuality.

The graphic imagery and messages displayed upon tote bags are becoming increasingly sophisticated and imaginative, as well as displaying the artist's sense of humour. Talented artists and designers are turning their hand to creating prints for tote bags; sometimes to promote their work, but also as commissioned projects from clients.

Artists and designers are using the medium of tote bags to help the world to become more environmentally conscious. But there is a potential pitfall for the tote's admirers: in trying to avoid plastic excess, we may end up owning too many totes! This is a potential threat to ponder while we jump on the bag-for-life bandwagon.

I hope you will enjoy this selection of imaginative and inspiring tote bags from individuals, collectives and design studios and that you may even be inspired to create your own tote bag artwork.

If you are interested in submitting your self-produced or commissioned projects for future editions of this book, please visit the Tote Prints blog (www.toteprints. wordpress.com).

Jitesh Patel, Jai Studio

Aaron D. Carámbula

Objective Subject

www.objectivesubject.com

Brooklyn, NY, USA

Have you ever heard of the Friends of Type? This is a daily type and lettering sketchbook made by Aaron Carámbula and his friends. His wife Kelly noticed the 'mmmm' design Aaron created for that project, and thought it would make a perfect design for the tote bag you see here.

Aaron runs the studio Objective Subject in Brooklyn, often using type and lettering at the centre of his designs. A declared fan and student of the Basel school, he designed

this tote bag print as a gift for the supporters of *Remedy Quarterly* food magazine. 'A tote made conceptual sense – functional at the greenmarket,' he comments. It also serves as a great high-value item, especially for designers, aesthetes and foodies.

Aaron sees the popularity of tote bags in terms of marketing power: a powerful combination between a functional marketing tool and the fashionable green movement.

Adam Augustyn

www.adamaugustyn.com

Brooklyn, NY, USA

Adam Augustyn is a graphic designer and illustrator, a self-declared optimist who enjoys the work he does. In this case, the job was creating an unconventional logo for Obama supporters, in a very bold and graphic style.

Adam Augustyn Design proposed this psychedelic green and white print as something 'utilitarian and reusable,' in harmony with President Obama's politics concerning the environment.

The pattern is made of letterforms that are not quite legible if you view the tote closely, but as you move to a certain distance, the name hidden in the forms becomes clear to the eye. The artist thinks that the symbol is more visually appealing when treated as an image.

Alícia Roselló
&
Elisa Riera

Sirena con Jersey

www.sirenaconjersey.com

Barcelona, Spain

'Sirena con Jersey' is the Spanish for 'mermaid with sweater'. Why would a mermaid wear a sweater? Because she wants to. Alícia Roselló and Elisa Riera, the women behind Sirena con Jersey, bring us a fresh perspective on creativity and lots of fun from Barcelona, Spain.

Ali and Eli have a unique personal style: 'We design what we would like to wear and that we don't find in stores. The "Mr Moustache" design looks slightly like the face on the Pringles chip tubes, but the resemblance was not intended! "Happy Worms" could be worms, fingers or whatever you like, and "Whale" is based on our love of whales and dolphins.'

Designing a tote bag seemed appealing to the young artists; 'it is unisex, is easy, is useful and we could do it ourselves,' they say.

Andre Weier

Nalindesign

www.nalindesign.com

Neuenrade, Germany

Simple black and white graphics define Andre Weier's design style when it comes to tote prints. His studio, Nalindesign, started to produce totes to fulfill personal needs: 'I and friends of mine just couldn't find great tote bags – so I started creating them myself,' he explains.

An admirer of street art, graffiti and urban style, Andre features various styles in his work, from typographic to urban. His love of stencils, spray paint and markers is also apparent in these totes. Andre says he is inspired by 'everything that surrounds me,' but mostly by human expressions. Upside down, smiling, grinning, his face tote bags are mainly used as giveaways for friends and clients.

Andre believes that the popularity of tote bags is due to their usefulness and their effectiveness in 'go green' campaigns. He thinks everybody needs one.

Andrea Forgacs

www.andreaforgacs.de

London, UK

If you think tote bags are a way of displaying design in everyday life, then you share an aesthetic vibe with illustrator Andrea Forgacs. She loves totes, owns more than twenty of them, and also makes them herself.

Her illustrations can't be pinned down to any one style, but Andrea suggests they are 'mostly innocent, with a little bit of black humour.'

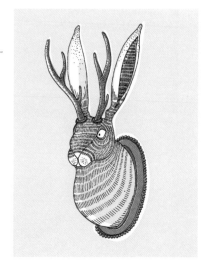

Andy Ainger

www.andyainger.com

London, UK

Tribal motifs and totemic symbols in neon pink and black make a lasting impression when placed on a white canvas. These striking hand-painted bags reflect Andy Ainger's distinctive style, an interesting combination of 'hand-rendered aesthetic and fun appearance,' in his own words. This style is constantly changing and developing as Andy takes inspiration from different fields, such as paper cutting.

The London-based illustrator produced these tote bags for a friend's market stall on Brick Lane. He had happened to draw characters with two sets of eyes a week or two before being asked to design the bags, so decided to put the characters on the totes.

Andy likes to see his designs developing spontaneously, without planning the finished look. But he admits that he wanted some graphic pieces to stand out among the rest of the bags on sale.

Andrew Bannecker

www.centralillustration.com

Washington, D.C., USA

Colourful backgrounds, peace symbols and slogans reminiscent of the Flower Power era: there's something hip about Andrew Bannecker's designs. Or should we say hippy?

The artist himself confirms an admiration for art from the 1960s, and describes his own style as 'lots of texture with a dash of whimsy.'

The Outfit in California, a company that collaborates with artists and designers to produce limited-edition bags, invited Andrew to create these tote bags. Even without having a specific audience in mind, the artist prefers to create something he loves in the hope that people will appreciate it.

This might just happen, as people have a drive to be more eco-friendly and hiring professionals like Bannecker to design for tote bags has contributed to their rise in popularity.

We'd better admire these designs while they are here; Andrew says he doesn't like to 'linger too long on any particular style, as I try to always be evolving.'

Angie McCarthy

Materialistic

www.materialistic.com.au

Sydney, Australia

Do you ever feel the need to say 'What a Lovely Tote!' when you see something that looks like the 'Best in Show'? Designer Angie McCarthy, owner of the Materialistic studio in Sydney, Australia, has you covered – these slogans feature on two of her vibrant, upbeat, typography-inspired tote bags.

Materialistic has the motto 'Lovely stuff you just have to have', and was created as the 'natural progression to a textile-loving, high heel-wearing, colour-obsessed designer with authority issues.'

Anke Weckmann

www.linotte.net

London, UK

When drawing is your favourite thing in the world, as Anke Weckmann says, it is only natural to illustrate nice things with nice characters. Even if you are a grown-up, why not carry with you images of childhood and innocence?

Anke draws characters ready to embellish a regular tote bag designed for a regular audience of girls and young women. Although she is now based in London, Anke's roots are German, and her work depicts the influence of her native fairy tales.

The tote bag shown above reveals this influence; from the first glance you may wonder in which story you have met that girl in her folk costume, as she seems both new and familiar at the same time.

Angus Hyland

Pentagram Design

www.pentagram.com

International: Austin, Berlin, London, New York, San Francisco

British artist Angus Hyland has won more than a hundred awards for his creative work. His designs may look simple, but they succeed in expressing the right message to the right audience.

Angus began collaborating with Cass Art, suppliers of artists' materials, in 2003, when he created their identity and packaging. These reusable bags are part of the company's promotion.

These totes are not only visually intriguing but also educational. Scarlet lake, viridian, phthalo turquoise and quinacridone magenta may be familiar terms for artists as names of paint colours, but these totes explain the terms to the rest of us so we learn a new language – the language of beautiful colours. The art lesson continues on the back of the tote, with an enumeration of various paintings, classic and modern, that use that particular colour.

The black and white totes 'Art in Transit' and 'Art in a Bag' feature bold writing on one side and iconographic symbols on the other. Among these you can recognize the silhouettes of famous sculptures, art supplies and artists' tools.

60's   80's   00's

Ashkahn

www.ashkahn.com

Los Angeles, CA, USA

'Perky' is not the usual adjective to associate with your regular tote bag. But an Ashkahn tote print is not exactly regular, either.

LA designer Ashkahn likes to amaze his audience with unusual designs. They feature bright colours and a 'raw, real and painfully humoristic' approach. The design featured here depicts the evolution of…um…hair styling in terms of women's choice through recent decades.

This can also be seen as an ecological graphic, as it reflects changes of hair style as a side effect of global warming (the greater the warming, the shorter the hair).

Ashkahn claims that his life experiences provided the source of inspiration for this tote print. There is only one thing to experience further: the reaction of his audience to the proposal of carrying groceries in this tote bag!

Ashley Jessiman

SodaKitsch

**www.sodakitsch.
supermarkethq.com**

Edinburgh, UK

Ashley Jessiman from SodaKitsch Studio offers leather versions of the tote. Like many other illustrators, Ashley regards the tote bag as 'a great platform for designers/illustrators to get their work out there and a great way for consumers to show off their personal style without spending lots of money.'

Ashley says she is influenced by indie designers. This nautical-themed design, with its clear, crisp lines, was inspired by the Scottish landscape. She thinks that 'nautical themes never seem to go out of fashion,' and that their popularity is not 'just with sailors and pirates'.

After all, have you seen any sailor or pirate carrying books and magazines in such a stylish tote?

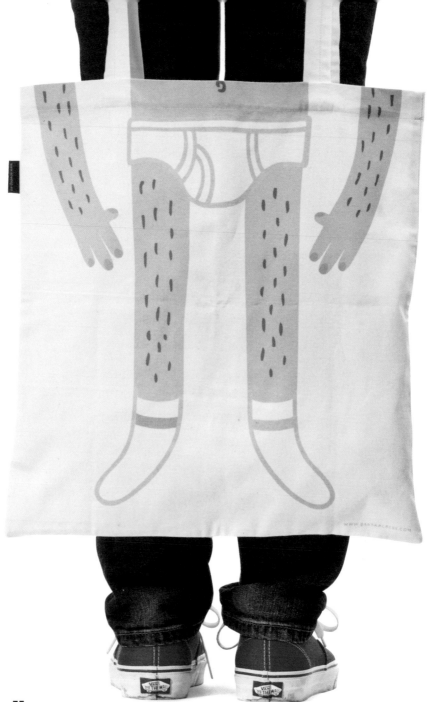

Bart Aalbers

www.bartaalbers.com

Rotterdam, The Netherlands

Anyone who likes a nice and slightly humorous tote bag will discover something to suit their taste in Bart Aalbers' portfolio – for instance, the 'Easy Does It' tote bag shown opposite, which Bart designed for textile retailer Envelop.eu, or the guy in tighty whities in the design above, with his message for modern, hurried, stressed people to chill out.

Bart's passion for drawing and illustrating began when he started helping out local bands in the Rotterdam area with their artwork and making flyers for gigs. His style influences include animation studio United Productions of America (UPA), vintage children's illustrations, cartoons and custom lettering, and he tries to find a balance of those influences in his own work.

Bart thinks the appeal of tote bags is that they 'are able to show what your interests are, much like T-shirts.' For this artist, the tote bag is an easy way to get his work onto the streets.

Becky Redman

www.beckyredman.com

London, UK

Images: simple. Statements: from the usual to the potentially offensive. Colours: not so many. Here's a designer who's not afraid to stick a message into one's face. Becky Redman's tote bags are meant to 'awaken a sense of wonder about one's environment' through the use of clean and simple layouts with slight abstractions of text.

Becky believes that a combination of simple commands and statistics increases the retention of information. Her prints are bold and arresting.

An admirer of post-punk culture, indie magazines and old-fashioned stuff, Becky used an informative style for these prints, trying to find the simplest way to tell it how it is and also be blunt. 'It's unconventional,' she thinks, 'but it grabs attention and provokes curiosity.'

Bosque Studio

www.holabosque.com.ar

Buenos Aires, Argentina

Bosque Studio is located in Buenos Aires, Argentina, and their illustrators like totes because 'they look funny and cute'. The team's aim is to generate simple graphics with an innovative way of using materials, mixing graphic design with art.

The designers think the tote bag is a great place to put a design that will be walking the streets. They prefer a simple graphic style, using shapes and colours with direct messages and a complex technique with an interesting background.

The limited-edition Bosque Studio products are hand-printed unique designs, full of colour, shapes, type, characters and simple life messages. They are aimed at people who want 'to use a unique work of art as a bag'. There's no reason for these totes to be left at home, as their purpose is to be used and carried everywhere.

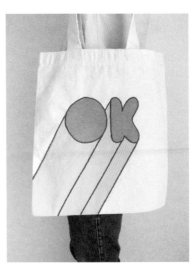

Bratislav
Milenkovic

www.bratislavmilenkovic.com

Belgrade, Serbia

Experimenting with typography and illustration, Serbian designer Bratislav Milenkovic makes a statement with this 'Fake Fur' tote bag, and it's written all over it. The idea came to him some time ago, when he saw some very expensive fur bags. They were the starting point for creating illustrations that had something to do with fur or fake fur. This type treatment illustration with vector fur is 'probably the fakest fur ever,' Bratislav jokes. This bag was produced in a limited edition.

Winner of various awards for illustration, typography and advertising concepts, Bratislav is currently on a postgraduate course in Advertising and Media. He also collaborates with various studios and agencies in Belgrade.

Bratislav thinks that tote bags have become popular over recent years because of their ability to be customized, the cool prints available, and their affordable price.

Carla & Hugo

Pinopaco

www.pinopaco.com

Lisbon, Portugal

You can always enjoy 'Green Flowers' without being a huge 'World Fan', but if you have two interesting, well-designed tote bag designs like these, you probably wear and like them both.

Carla and Hugo, the Pinopaco team from Portugal, offer wearable designs that are 'fun and full of sub-layers'. Nature and global unity is what they stand for, and it seems to work just fine, as 'plastic bags are finally (and slowly) disappearing, and everyone is starting to use eco-friendly alternatives' (at least in Lisbon).

The choice between plastic and cotton is easier than you think when tote bags come with such pretty images, simple colours, effective symbols, and fresh, attractive prints.

Pinopaco use creativity with a social purpose, drawing nature-inspired themes in order to become useful to our environment. If we care about the environment, we can use the tote bag as 'a blank canvas full of graphic capabilities to explore, and a great way to communicate.'

Caroline Roach

Champ + Rosie

www.champandrosie.com.au

Perth, Australia

Champ + Rosie = Caroline Roach, an Australian designer who admires 'thought out and understated' European artwork and creates cute, minimalist tote bag designs. Black owls, robots and elephants on white canvas feature in her designs. The totes combine the functional and the beautiful, or, as Caroline likes to describe it, 'fun and cute things; a little sweet to escape the daily grind.'

Having a bag obsession, as addict Caroline admits, she 'found it hard to find bags with printed graphics' to really enjoy. This marked the beginning of a beautiful adventure, as she decided to create her own designs.

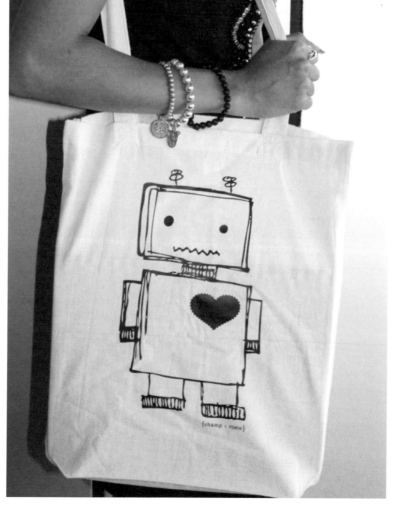

Catalina Estrada
for Purocorazón

Purocorazón S.A.C.

www.mipurocorazon.com

Lima, Peru

This tote print, one of a series for Peruvian homeware company Purocorazón, depicts the stylized story of a romance between a puma and a cockatoo, based on an illustration by artist Catalina Estrada. Expert Peruvian craftspeople from various parts of the country added embroidery embellishments typical of each location, creating new versions of the project with each interpretation. Cross-stitching, ribbon-lined borders and patchwork were some of the techniques used to add vitality and freshness to the designs.

The optimistic colour scheme gives the story the light-hearted touch that also characterizes Peruvian craftsmanship.

The message of the totes is happiness, love of colour, of form, of traditional art and also a belief in equality, as the imagination can't be limited by borders.

Central Illustration Agency

www.centralillustration.com

London, UK

Central Illustration Agency (C.I.A.) represents many illustrators and artists, demonstrating a love of variety and openness to unconventional ways of artistic expression. From exhibitions, art and illustration shows, to beautifully printed ephemera, the agency showcases a style that reflects 'modern-day technology with a mix of tradition and the hand-rendered.'

C.I.A. started producing totes a few years ago for fans, clients and customers. They wanted them to stand out and be of high and sustainable quality. Art legend Sir Peter Blake designed the first tote in 2007, which was given away to all attendees of that year's Consequences Show. In 2008, the agency signed the talented Andrew Bannecker (see p. 14), who was invited to create a second tote design, pictured below.

C.I.A. sees the tote as a 'response to sustainable living, thinking about the environment.' Totes have also become part of contemporary fashion and culture, as they have evolved into something like 'art on a shopping bag, which is much more affordable.'

Chris Judge

www.chrisjudge.com

Dublin, Ireland

Sometimes we'd love to know what is on other people's minds, even without their approval. Chris Judge gives us a perfectly legal and moral way to have a glimpse at 'the ideas people store in their heads all day bursting forth from their minds.'

He's not a weird scientist, but an illustrator and painter responsible for the design of this tote print, 'Inside Out'. The Dublin-based artist depicts in a fun and colourful style a multitude of symbols for the ideas springing from a man's head, on a starry background.

Chris's style is a modern interpretation of the comic-book style, a tribute to American illustrators of the 1950s and 60s with a touch of humour. It is 'a little bit cute and a little bit weird,' as Chris himself says.

Chris Piascik

www.chrispiascik.com

Boston, MA, USA

We can talk about protecting the planet all day long, but sometimes a good image is worth more than any words. Chris Piascik's print design is eloquent simply with the silhouettes of all those marine creatures, but it also spells out a thankful message.

'My work is illustrative, usually improvised and often incorporates loose lettering styles,' says the graphic artist from Boston. The inspiration for this tote came after Chris read an article about how many sea creatures are killed because of discarded plastic bags. He thought of a design that would communicate to less ecologically aware people, but 'ironically, the people who bought it were already conscious of the environment.'

With its 'cute, yet passive-aggressive way to make people consider the damage plastic bags can cause,' Chris Piascik's loose illustrative style delivers a powerful message you can hardly ignore.

Colm Larkin

Airside

www.airside.co.uk

London, UK

Airside is a creative agency whose designers have the opportunity to express themselves away from the demands of clients and deadlines. Most of Airside Shop's customers are male T-shirt fans, but their unique approach sometimes appeals to women too.

In the beginning, tote bags were made by people in the studio just for themselves. Their designs take inspiration from sources like environmental issues ('Hey! I Give a Damn') or an anti-Valentine's Day attitude ('I'm Not In Love'), among others.

Christopher & Kathleen Sleboda

Part of It

www.partofit.org

Guilford, CT, USA

Concerned about how to make a better world? Launched in 2007 by Christopher and Kathleen Sleboda (also known as graphic-making team Gluekit), the Part of It project uses artists to help change attitudes to various causes, making activism 'fun, personal, beautiful and engaging.' Fifteen designers and artists (including Garrett Morin, Wyeth Hansen, Dustin Amery Hostetler, Adrian Johnson, Mark Owens, Michael Perry and Ryan Waller) have already joined the efforts and depicted their favourite causes on tote bags.

From typographic to image-driven style, there are many ways to represent the various issues important to the Part of It collective. Whether it is a message of protest or a simple declaration, sweet and touchy, bold and cool, elaborate or minimalist, every design has its own power in making a difference in the world.

Along with the Part of It T-shirts, the tote bags are a fashionable means to express the right statements to thoughtful consumers with good design sensibilities. When the totes display a visual expression of people's belief in positive change, they are even better than a simple fashion object.

Top row, left to right:

Genevieve Gauckler, 'Harmony Nature Future'

Jim Datz, 'No Grief For My Reef'

Garrett Morin, 'Drive You Home'

DIY, 'Rebuild'

Bottom row, left to right:

Ryan Waller, 'Library'

Ken Meier & David Yun, 'Let's Be Honest'

Mark Owens, 'Inherit The Wind'

Justin Fines, 'Smile'

From top to bottom:

Dustin Amery Hostetler,
'Make Art Now'

Adrian Johnson,
'Resistance is Fertile'

Wyeth Hansen,
'Make Some Noise'

From top to bottom:

Daniel Eatock, 'Alphabet'

Genevieve Gauckler,
'Save Polar Bears'

Ryan Waller, 'Museum'

Claudia Brown
& Jessie Whipple
Vickery

Pattern People

www.patternpeople.com

Portland, OR, USA

What do Karl Lagerfeld, Marc Jacobs, Michael Jackson and Prince have in common? At least one thing: the Tribute Totes made by Pattern People.

The US company's design duo, Claudia Brown and Jessie Whipple Vickery, found this gesture a way to show off their intricate and sometimes psychedelic design style. They also see tote bags as a great blank canvas on which to show off their illustrations. They immersed themselves in the symbols associated with the above-mentioned VIPs and chose the most iconic objects associated with them to illustrate the totes.

Why totes? For many reasons, 'from being eco-friendly to simply having too much to carry in everyday life,' they say. That means appealing to fashion lovers and music lovers everywhere, in order to raise awareness that 'a reusable tote bag is a great solution to the waste created with disposable bags.'

Dave Hughes

Ammo Magazine

www.ammomagazine.co.uk

Birmingham, UK

The ghetto blaster illustration here was not originally intended as a bag design. Created by Dave Hughes as part of a personal printed project, *Koodoo Magazine*, it came to the attention of Cut-Out, a screenprinter who runs a fashion label, who felt Dave's illustrations would be perfect for printing on bags and T-shirts.

The 'Cake Club' design above, intended to be bright, fun and eye-catching, was one of the first screenprinted products for *Ammo*.

Dave says he is a fan of artwork that 'has been created purely for enjoyment, and that the creator has a personal passion for.'

David Denosowicz & Maggie Doyle

Loyalty & Blood

www.loyaltyandblood.com

Brooklyn, NY, USA

Do you like monograms? Old typography? Or blood-written statements? Apparently so do David Denosowicz and Maggie Doyle, the Loyalty & Blood husband-and-wife team from New York. 'We love hand-drawn, quirky images, menacing photographs, and things that most people find silly,' they comment.

It is not difficult to see that ancient art is a source of inspiration for the duo, and it is also obvious that they mix styles in their own way. Their collection of tote bags initially started through an obsession for typography. Their other inspirations include music, animals, doodles on napkins, New York City galleries and museums, and their own collection of art magazines and books.

Dom Murphy

TAK!

www.taktak.net

Birmingham, UK

Offering clean and contemporary style with playful zest, the inspiration for this tote bag was the typeface featured in the design. Called Woodland, the type was created by Dom Murphy at TAK! design agency and is made of letters shaped like individual animals, from birds to hedgehogs.

The tote was originally made with friends and family in mind, but it is also offered (with promotional material) to clients of TAK!

From an ecological point of view, the tote bag has become as interesting as the T-shirt; it has a role not just in carrying groceries, but also in communicating messages about being green. This bag can also double its function and be used as a record bag when vinyl-hunting.

eBoy

www.hello.eboy.com

Berlin, Germany

If you were concerned that modern designers usually target women for their products, breathe a sigh of relief; men also have their fair share of nice stuff from creative studios like eBoy, including tote bags and other eco-friendly products.

This colourful tote bag was designed by eBoy for the Gola sports brand. Inspiration came from their love of totes, considered by this creative masculine trio as 'the archetype of a bag'. Like many other designers, they think that tote bags offer the ideal blank canvas for designs.

What is the design of this Gola L.A. limited-edition bag about? Funky colours and shapes, comic books and of course the city of L.A. itself, 'the perfect city for tote baggin'.' The city is also the main character featured in this urban-inspired bag.

Elena Gallen

www.elenagallen.com

Barcelona, Spain

Dark, iconic, conceptual – this is how designer Elena Gallen describes her artwork. Elena says she admires 'classic fashion designers with good taste and nice garments,' but her own style is mostly on the 'minority, odd and clever' side.

Trying to explore new media, Elena applied her most renowned T-shirt print, 'Oh My Coke', to a tote bag. The print features model Kate Moss with a bleeding nose to portray the celebrity's reported cocaine use.

Elena explains, 'Luxury & Trash, the collection that contains this design, is a compilation of illustration prints of controversial celebrities. I personalized the praise and the criticism put on certain celebrities and, by extension, on the society that praises such imperfect idols.'

As for the tote, Elena likes it as a medium because it is 'simple, cheap, comfy and a great canvas for art prints.'

Erika Firm

Delphine

www.delphinepress.com

Delphine, CA, USA

Erika Firm's designs are joyful, brightly coloured, summery and optimistic. The graphic artist from California likes bold, whimsical and simple artwork and thinks that she has a vintage-inspired style 'with a decidedly modern twist.'

Erika's motivation for producing totes was that 'stores usually give out boring tote bags, and if we have to go through all the grocery shopping, we may as well do so with a cute bag on our arms.' This is true for many women, especially southern Californians, whom Erika initially had in mind when creating these prints.

The designs are inspired by the 'natural beauty of the great outdoors in California.' The bags have strong eco credentials too, being made from 80 per cent recycled cotton and 20 per cent recycled plastic bottles.

Fabian Monheim

Fly Productions

www.fly-production.com

London, UK

'I love the spirit of the 1950s and 60s as a period in which a lot of designers created work that has been driven by a contemporary philosophy,' says graphic artist Fabian Monheim. His style of work remixes the things he finds into something new.

Fita Frattini Caica

fitafrattini@gmail.com

Santiago, Chile

When inspiration comes, with 'the candies, with drawings of my childhood and things that make me laugh and what I like to see,' as it happens for designer Fita Frattini Caica, nice things come out of this combination – tote bags, for instance.

Fita wanted to try different things, including translating her simple, fun pictures into the area of textiles. Working with collage, overlays and transparencies, Fita wanted to try something different and – because 'inspiration is somewhat difficult to control' – the result is what you see here.

The creation of these handmade silkscreened tote bags was exactly how a creation should be: free and almost unplanned by the artist, and interesting to see and to wear for the general public.

Fita thinks that the use of totes may help us to 'recover the sense of the value of simple things.'

Gabe Wong

www.gabewong.ca

Edmonton, Canada

What would you do to support the planet and make people more environmentally conscious? If you are a designer, illustrator, project-maker and all-around creative guy, like Gabe Wong, you'd probably say 'yes' to spreading positive influence.

His positive influence was utilized by University of Alberta student group Environmental Coordination Office of Students (ECOS), who wanted to make their campus a more sustainable place. They asked Gabe to design a bag for them, displaying ECOS' motto. The result: a practical two-colour print on a cream cotton tote bag, called 'Keeping it Green'.

Gabrijela Bulatovic

wizards@nadlanu.com

Belgrade, Serbia

Everybody likes monsters when they are cute and live on tote bags. Gabrijela Bulatovic's Monsters project is one of these happy cases. The Serbian designer created a bag 'that is functional and has a character', and is entirely handmade, from the sewing to the linocut print.

Gabrijela doesn't define the style she most admires; she simply likes designs that are 'expressive and full of all art elements'. Her own designs can be described as freestyle; she

says, 'I use different techniques depending on how I feel at a given moment or how it contributes to the theme I am working on.'

Gabrijela chose the tote bag as a form of expression, as a 'message you can wear around on your shoulder.' And to paraphrase Gabrijela's favourite *Snoopy* episode, 'Everywhere you go, always take your monster with you.'

Gemma Busquets

www.gemmabusquets.com

Barcelona, Spain

Designing something that is simple, understandable, with a concept behind it and that everybody could wear is not an easy thing to do, but that is what graphic artist Gemma Busquets tries to achieve with her tote prints.

Trendy, ecological and aesthetic, her tote bags have won the hearts of many admirers with their simple, unpretentious style.

Gemma Correll

www.gemmacorrell.com

Norwich, UK

Pug lovers and tandem fans can now enjoy a practical and affordable tote that reflects their tastes, by choosing one of Gemma Correll's prints.

Gemma, an admirer of both hand-drawn and screenprinted illustrations, has a taste for simple, naive graphics, and her own style reflects this. She created the tote prints 'Let's Ride' and 'Pugs Not Drugs' for a wide range of people, even though it seems that her work appeals more to females than males. The audience she aims for is people who appreciate 'some degree of intelligence,' and not only the cute graphics.

Gemma Latimer

www.gemmalatimer.com

London, UK

Tired of your old tote bag? Here's something to keep your eyes wide open for a while – the fascinating combinations of human and animal elements in Gemma Latimer's black and white designs.

'Teapot Man', 'Clownbird', 'Cowchap', and 'Birdman' come from a fantastic collage gallery created by Gemma. The characters were first featured in a project exploring 'the eccentricities of what it is to be British.'

Why use collage? Gemma thinks it has 'a certain tangibility, a quality that cannot be captured by digital means alone.' She combines past and present, illustration and photography, and fantasy and reality in a unique manner. She eventually translates her designs to the blank canvas of the tote bag, transporting the artworks to the modern world.

So, if you like a good dose of 'circuses, Victoriana and surrealism' in your life, you're probably ready to let one of Gemma's designs become your own means of self-expression.

Gemma Shiel

Lazy Oaf

www.lazyoaf.co.uk

London, UK

Do you love designs with a bit of humour and fun? So does Gemma Shiel of Lazy Oaf. Her own designs are a combination of 'low-fi illustrations, bright colours and bold prints with a little wink,' as she likes to describe them.

These tote bag designs sprang from a variety of inspirations. The 'Loafer' design was simply a dedication to the artist's favourite type of slip-on shoe. The red 'Happy/Sad' tote bag was inspired by the Lazy Oaf reversible sweatshirt, which allows you to switch sides depending on your mood. Keep yourself well and truly disguised with 'Groucho', while 'Beatbox Boy' gets the party started wherever you go.

Gemma thinks a tote bag is 'a great shape for a print design,' something that allows you to carry things, and an accessory 'you don't need to plan an outfit around!'

GraphicAirlines

GraphicAirlines Design & Creative

www.graphicairlines.com

Hong Kong

Have you ever thought that ugliness could be interesting enough to make the subject of a tote bag? GraphicAirlines has.

Created for a mostly female audience, these simple, affordable, yet nice-looking products are designed to appeal to those who have had enough of cuteness. And let's not forget that modern Asian cultural productions practically introduced cuteness to the world market…

GraphicAirlines's distinctive style practises the 'aesthetics of ugly'. As the design studio states, 'cute we are not.' Instead, they create poignant patterns in minimalist colour schemes, unusual characters and unlikely contexts. Plump-cheeked children and adults, riding pugs or rabbits, kind of hilarious yet a little scary, are typical features of the designs.

Hanna Melin

www.hannamelin.com

London, UK

A great admirer of designers and artists who mix materials into 'something new and exciting that you didn't think was possible,' Hanna Melin describes her own style in just one word: fun.

Fun outdoor activities, people having a nice time – looks like summer to me! A bit of nostalgia, images of old audio tapes (where did those years go?), and the picture is complete. Hanna Melin finds inspiration in personal memories; joyful ones, yet with a certain wistfulness.

Hannah Goudge

The Gild

www.the-gild.com

London, UK

There's something clever about a tote bag that states something you wouldn't see at first sight. Instead of using a traditional green colour to express a 'green' message, Hannah Goudge of The Gild has chosen a creative way to express an eco message. Playful language makes the tote eye-catching, and the two-sided print also grabs interest.

Hannah designed this tote print for Virgin Trains, as the company wanted to highlight its green credentials 'in an unobvious, playful way.' The bag was addressed mainly to the company's employees, but it can appeal to anyone.

Hannah describes her style of work as playful, colourful and clean, as is apparent in this red and white design with its bold typography.

Hannah Chipkin

Chip Chop!

www.chipchop.com.au

Melbourne, Australia

Playful, humorous, charming – Australian designer Hannah Chipkin's totes are eye candy in the world of white canvas. Typography in pleasant colours and an inspired choice of words define her Chip Chop! products.

Hannah is drawn to 'bold colour, interesting textures, prints, typography and eccentric detail,' which she uses for the aesthetic signature of her designs. 'Fun and mischief combine with bold yet simple typography, block colour and good-quality fabrics,' she comments.

Because the bags Hannah designs are usually 'more out-there than the T-shirts,' helping customers get noticed, she chooses statements inspired by 'beautiful things, pop culture, film, typography, art, icons, fashion, word play, anything French.'

Hannah thinks the tote bag has opened up another form of self-expression, so she likes to design 'fashion with brains'. On the other hand, totes are popular eco items and useful products into which you could fit 'everything you could possibly need for a day out.'

Hannah Stouffer

www.grandarray.com

Los Angeles, CA, USA

How can psychedelic, satanic and classy share the same canvas? We'd better ask designer Hannah Stouffer that question, as she tries to combine all those elements in her work. Her style is showcased by her tote prints, made under the name of Grand*Array, a Los Angeles-based studio.

Generally drawn to linework in art and clean, classic lines, Hannah chose the tote bag as a means of expression in order to make 'a great product for illustration and design to be presented on, that isn't a T-shirt.' Her inspiration came from the concept of 'darkness within the light,' and she came up with a product for friends and all those people with similar interests to her own.

Hannah's bags are truly eye-catching. They direct your attention to a personal imaginary world where snakes, dragons, roses, kings and queens can live together, reminding you of Alice's journey in Wonderland.

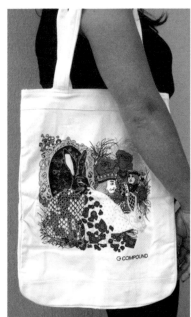

Hen Weekend

www.henweekend.org

UK

Hen Weekend is a networking organization set up by artist Ellie Harrison, with events aiming to facilitate discussion and encourage collaboration between its participants.

This tote bag was produced for the launch of a Hen Weekend event for female artists, writers and curators from around the UK and abroad.

The brief for the Hen Weekend logo design given to Eleanor Grosch was to be bold and empowering, creating a positive image that people

participating in the event could identify with. They did not want anything too stereotypically 'girly'.

The Hen Weekend bags were given away as a lasting souvenir for those who took part in the weekend.

Ellie Harrison says, 'tote bags became popular because of the justified environmental backlash against plastic.'

Hideo Kawamura

Kawamura Hideo Activity/Rezon

www.kha.jp/rezon

Tokyo, Japan

Modern cultural productions show us a lot of fierce characters who can transform themselves into warriors whenever something threatening happens. This is also the case with this bag. It may look like a 100 per cent cotton bag to you, with a certain Picasso touch, featuring a guy with a tote on his head. For the artist Hideo Kawamura, however, this is the ultimate 'Eco Warrior' bag, and it has a message for all those who pretend to be environmental activists.

If you see inconsiderate people throwing cigarette butts into the street, or not separating their rubbish by type, transform yourself into an eco warrior!

Hideo wanted to create a bag that has its own story, for people who are not that interested in the environment, but might be attracted by the idea of putting the bag on their head and wearing it like a mask. 'Anyone can be a hero,' he comments.

HUGE

www.hugeinc.com

Brooklyn, NY, USA

If you want to make a statement but words don't come easy, tote bags signed by HUGE may help. You can choose between 'Buy Me a Drink', 'I'm a Designer' and 'Gold, Weed, Money', among others.

The inspiration for the 'Buy Me a Drink' bag came from airport bars. The Huge designers dedicated this print to people sitting on their own, thinking that they could use an ice-breaker like this to invite other people over and engage in conversation.

The original design of the second simply said 'I'm a better designer than you,' but the designers crossed out 'better' and 'than you.' It now just says, 'I'm a designer', leaving the message open to interpretation between ego and humility.

Finally, 'the idea of letting people know what's in your tote bag, so they don't have to guess' led to the design of the 'Gold, Weed, Money' bag – as a joke, presumably!

Ian Stevenson

www.ianstevenson.co.uk

London, UK

Whimsical black and white puppets, smiling and moving, are set against a contrasting white canvas – Ian Stevenson's design exposes his 'mind and thoughts in a world of drawings.'

This tote was made for Blunt, a London-based agency representing illustrators and photographers. Ian Stevenson took the original artwork from a canvas that he had previously created at a live drawing event and gave it a new meaning.

Ian enjoys work that clearly communicates ideas, drawing not only on tote bags, but on walls, floors, rubbish and anything else he can find. Of course, tote bags are a great alternative to plastic bags and a good choice for Ian's 'odd world of distorted characters.'

This design wasn't targeted at any specific audience; the artist simply does his work hoping that people will enjoy it and 'the everyday strangeness of people and the world around' in a bright, cheery way.

Ingrid Reithaug
& Tonje Holand

Darling Clementine

www.darlingclementine.no

Oslo, Norway

Norway's Darling Clementine studio showcases the work of artists Ingrid Reithaug and Tonje Holand. They like to share their thoughts through design, and their creations are easy to understand for those who enjoy the simple style. They take their inspiration from classic Bauhaus, the illustrations of Paul Rand, Pierrot costumes and Disney animations.

What would be the artists' reasons for designing tote prints? They say they wanted to explore a different medium from their usual one of paper. They also wanted to move away from the computer. The final products feature fun designs and offer an environmentally friendly alternative to plastic bags.

Ingrid and Tonje also wanted to make people smile, so they used quirky characters, such as Monsieur Cabaret, and designs and symbols inspired by circus imagery and Grimm fairy tales.

Jason Ponggasam
& Patty Variboa

Fat Rabbit Farm

www.fatrabbitfarm.com

Los Angeles, CA, USA

Are you influenced by Japanese animations and all things fluffy? Then you'll probably enjoy these character-based totes from Fat Rabbit Farm. Designers Jason Ponggasam and Patty Variboa from Los Angeles try to 'give life and personality to everyday objects with big googly eyes and happy expressions.'

The characters include cows, bears, rabbits, and also strawberries, ice creams and cupcakes. Drawn in a simple, clean style, the characters are full of life, have friends and enemies, and are involved in different activities. The colours are friendly, and unexpected elements pop out from time to time, such as a polka-dot pink ribbon on a green canvas.

These totes were created for everyday use. They are aimed at anyone who loves and appreciates these particular fat bunnies.

Like the artists they admire, the designers of Fat Rabbit Farm create things that 'give off a positive feeling when you see them.'

Jason Scuderi

Antimotion

www.anti-motion.com

NY, USA

'From very simple illustrated graphics to sophisticated mental garbage,' New York-based artist Jason Scuderi from Antimotion likes to attack the rules of what we perceive to be the 'right way'. He also likes artists who dare to try something new in their field of creation.

Jason believes that tote bags serve 'a utilitarian purpose and can promote a message to social masses.' He thinks of the tote bag as the new T-shirt.

Jason's designs are characterized by a refreshing graphic simplicity and also a fun vibe. The themes are versatile, from a repetitive red and white pattern, to a happy cloud pouring rain, to a photographic representation of a smiling plastic bag. There are no complicated colour schemes and no intricate shapes and stories here, just a tote and its effective graphic design.

Jeremyville

www.jeremyville.com

Sydney, Australia

Jeremyville designs contain explicit ecological messages and cute, friendly, green and powerful graphics. With a unique voice, 'the Jeremyville style' is also present in animation, toys, murals, books, product design and apparel.

The designer says that no strategy or rational thought went into creating the tote prints; instead, intuition and feelings are involved. The hand-drawn designs add a casual feel.

Jitesh Patel

www.jiteshpatel.co.uk

London, UK

Intricate details and stunning black and white graphics make Jitesh Patel's designs edgy and suitable for 'people who would like to use and look cool with' the totes. His style of work is very decorative, as he likes to create work that is pleasing to the eye and well balanced.

'My ethos is always to try and create something better then the last piece of work,' says Jitesh. He believes that tote bags' popularity is due to an increasing eco-consciousness.

Joe Rogers

Colourbox

www.colourboxonline.com

Worcestershire, UK

What does a designer have in mind when creating something? I'm pretty sure it's something interesting, and Colourbox's Joe Rogers agrees, even though he has forgotten the inspiration that was whizzing around when creating these prints. They weren't aimed at a specific audience, just people 'out there that have the same taste as me,' says Joe.

Taking inspiration from all areas of art and design and beyond, Joe likes to mix the digital with the traditional. His tote bags, which feature bold statements with colours that can't pass unnoticed, are hand-screenprinted and produced as a promotional tool for his artwork.

Joe thinks the appeal of tote bags is that they are stronger than plastic bags, longer-lasting, easy to carry around, easy to fold up, and highly reusable. They are a fashion accessory, but also an item 'that shows a bit of your personality and taste to the world.'

John McFaul, Ollie Munden & Chris Malbon

McFaul Studio

www.mcfaulstudio.com

Chichester, UK

UK-based McFaul Studio has a design team comprised of three artists. They take influences from a variety of sources, from Pre-Raphaelite painters to today's finest Japanese tattoo artists. They play with design in an 'intricate, thoughtful, considered, colourful, detailed' and fresh-eyed style.

McFaul Studio are aware that in recent years artists have been using tote bags both as promotional items and to help the world become more environmentally conscious. Their own tote bag designs feature eco-friendly messages and imagery. The illustrations focus on nature and wildlife, reminding us to be more careful with the world and to 'treat the globe as our friend'.

The colour combinations and shapes of the bags are quite soft, with a feminine edge, but they also feature a strong graphic style that uses modern technology.

If you want to help the environment in a fashionable and stylish way, you are thinking the same way as McFaul Studio.

John Derian

John Derian Company

www.johnderian.com

Manhattan, NY, USA

John Derian's shop in New York City hosts beautiful items from a variety of artists, including these charming black-on-white designs by Hugo Guinness.

With their sharp and elegant graphic style, these tote bags make you wonder how something as simple as strong graphics on white canvas can combine to form such interesting work. These tote bags really rise to the status of works of art.

Jon Burgerman

www.jonburgerman.com

Nottingham, UK

Vibrant characters, always in some kind of motion, urban shapes inspired by Cubism, designs in clean colour schemes (mainly blue and pink) in a 'wonky, wibbly, odd, happy and dumb' style' – yes, we are talking about Jon Burgerman's totes. Actually, it is almost impossible to describe his style in a few words, as it is so versatile and surprising.

One of England's most famous cartoonists, Jon Burgerman describes his tote bag designs as featuring his 'looping lines that chime and rhyme.' He creates tote prints for clients including Dooperdoo, Sky Arts and Boosy, and tries to make the bags both pretty and useful.

Jon Knox

Hello, Brute

www.hellobrute.com

Portland, OR, USA

Black on white, white on black, a 'Caffeinated Jeffrey' or 'Boy Germs': there's no doubt about it, it must be something signed by Hello, Brute. Who is actually under this name, behind the 'emaciated models with weird bodies and ugly faces' and 'middle school yearbook, bored teenager' inspiration? The artist comes from the USA and his name is Jon Knox.

'Boy Germs' is printed in black on a raw canvas tote. The design is based on a graphite drawing from an ongoing series of portraits blending Jon's drawn characters with images of children.

'Caffeinated Jeffrey' features Jon's character Jeffrey, an annoying rabbit who is always jacked up on caffeine. This design is also printed in one colour – white on a black tote.

Jon put his designs on tote bags because 'they are versatile and affordable, allowing people to own quite a few, and they're easy on the environment.' The artist adds that he designs and produces stuff that he likes and that he uses himself.

Jon Simmons

www.jon-simmons.co.uk

Leeds, UK

Jon Simmons' 'T Bag' is a simple, striking composition signed by the Leeds-based graphic artist.

Jon is very fond of minimal, bold design, but also of 1920s graphic design, tattooing and all things typographic. The designer says he loves to 'explore the crossover between typography, illustration and photography in various ways, some subtle, some not.'

The inspiration for this tote print arose during one of Jon's regular tea breaks at work. He then used his bold style of making 'intriguing graphics for any occasion' to put the design on canvas.

Josephine Ada Chinonye Chime

www.adachinonye.com

London, UK

London-based artist and sculptor Josephine Ada Chinonye Chime likes to explore different subject matters and topics. These two bags were based on sculptures that explored the identity of the self. Josephine finds physical imperfections such as bumps, lumps, pimples and dimples beautiful and exhilarating to draw. The artist wanted to expose what people find 'ugly', making 'ugly' open for people to see and strike up a dialogue about.

Josephine sees tote bags as a walking billboard; 'it's a great way to get images or information seen by various people, and is cost-effective.'

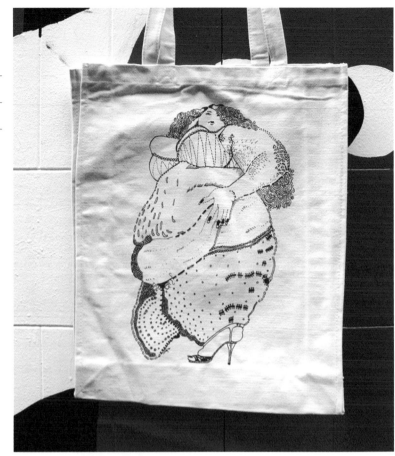

Josh Cochran

www.joshcochran.net

Brooklyn, NY, USA

Graphic artist Josh Cochran has an innovative take on tote bag prints. Take these two designs, for instance, where he tried to do 'something interesting and different from the generic totes most people use.' The 'Nietzsche' tote design was previously used as a graphic for an editorial assignment for the *New York Times*. The 'Jellyfish' tote bag was inspired by 'the most amazing fluorescent jellyfish,' which Josh saw in an aquarium in Osaka, Japan.

Whether you are interested in sea life or fascinated by modern philosophy, these totes give you the opportunity to wear your favourite subject on your shoulder.

Julia Nielsen

www.pryldesign.se

Stockholm, Sweden

Julia Nielsen's bags are Hipp! and that's more than the name of the Swedish brand she designed them for. They are also colourful and meticulous. For Julia, tote bags are an environment where joyful animal prints would feel at home. She saw the commission as a good challenge to create a family of animals that would look good on your shoulder.

Julia Pott

www.juliapott.com

London, UK

Nature has both impressive and cute things to show us, but sometimes we forget about all the beauties around. A little more awareness and a screenprinted canvas bag like this one from Julia Pott are good ways of bringing them to our attention.

The London-based freelance illustrator/animator uses this tote bag to depict a black-and-white image of 'a big burly bear holding a small bush baby'. But there's more meaning behind what we see at first glance.

'The idea behind the work is that of the comfort of being with someone else, but also the constant underlying feeling of losing them,' the artist explains.

Plain and simple, the design is less focused on colours and shapes and more on expressing an idea.

Julie Courtois

juliluli.blogspot.com

Montréal, Canada

So far there have been many attempts to create universal languages, such as Esperanto, but artist Julie Courtois proposes a more interesting one – the green language.

How does she do that? With the help of an inspired design, 'making a statement about the global issue of the environment without coming across as too preachy.'

The Canadian graphic designer finds inspiration in 'everyday life, music, nature, food, fashion.' She is also a big fan of cartoons and comic strips by both European and Asian artists.

This tote design looks like the work of an eco-thinking person. The world Julie envisions is 'full of sweets and puppies'. The idea behind the design was to produce a green item that was 'hip and trendy but also versatile and accessible to a variety of people.'

Whether in a chic downtown shop, bookstore, café or just an everyday market, the bag would send a message about being green.

Kai Clements &
Anthony Sunter

Kai and Sunny

www.kaiandsunny.com

Brighton, UK

Kai and Sunny (Kai Clements and Anthony Sunter) are graphic designers. They are inspired by many contemporary designers and artists, but their biggest influence comes from nature. Their illustrations have a bold graphic style and they believe that tote bags are useful for increasing interest in recycling.

Kay and Sunny designed this tote bag as part of a press pack for McQ by Alexander McQueen's spring 2010 collection. The pack also included a T-shirt and a CD by Unkle.

The inspiration for the design came from one of the prints in the collection, which had a broken glass pattern.

Kalene Rivers & Dan Weise

Open Space/Thundercut

www.openspacebeacon.com

Beacon, NY, USA

Sometimes, if they are really inspiring, tote bags become art gallery items. Curators Kalene Rivers and Dan Weise from Open Space/Thundercut gallery showcase the works of a very diverse group of creative people. The collection concentrates on the subculture contemporary art movement: street culture, urban environments, independent music, architecture, graphic design, illustration and, of course, tote prints.

The gallery hosted an exhibition during which totes were sold to benefit an environmental charity. 'The Tote Bag show was inspired by the need to be more environmentally minded in the world today,' say the curators. More than a hundred global artists donated their time and talent in the form of custom-designed tote bags.

Many unique visions and concepts can be spotted in these totes. Prints, illustrations, drawings, sewing and patching were the weapons used in raising people's awareness in this peaceful and aesthetic protest.

Top row, left to right:

Open Space (two images)

Caroline Hwang

Bottom row, left to right:

Jim Darling

Starla Petersen

Fernada Cohen (two images)

Top row, left to right:

Ian Stevenson

Chris Dickason

C215

Triboro

Bottom row, left to right:

BO130

Blutt

Dick

August Heffner

Karin Söderquist

www.karinsoderquist.com

London, UK

Karin Söderquist likes pop music, vegetarian sushi, North Pole explorers and drawing (of course). The graphic artist lives in London, designs T-shirts, record sleeves and wallets for clients, and she designed this tote print, too.

Playful, clean and naive, a crying bear head looks at us from the tote canvas. 'I've had a thing for polar bears since I was a kid,' says the Swedish artist, who is now worried about global warming shrinking polar bears' habitats and threatening them with extinction. The inspiration for this print was the thought of polar bears disappearing.

Karin regards tote bags as practical items, mostly affordable and a great way of displaying nice designs. Using and loving tote bags for a long time made it natural for Karin to design one herself, 'for someone who's got the same taste for cute things' as her.

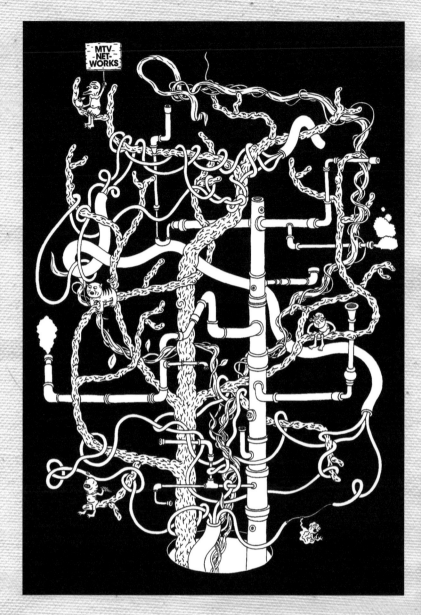

Karl Grandin &
Björn Atldax

Vår

www.vaar.se

Stockholm, Sweden

Karl Grandin and Björn Atldax joined forces in 1996 to work on both personal and commercial art projects from their studio in Stockholm, Sweden. The two were responsible for the graphic expression for Cheap Monday, a clothing label started by some friends in 2004.

As people who admire 'art that defies definition,' they declare themselves stunned by the fantastic imagery created by the sixteenth-century painter Hieronymus Bosch, but also by local graffiti writers.

Their own style illustrates concepts that are in between or beyond what is usual art, using combinations of fragments, a cut-and-paste of ideas as well as images, bringing together high, pop and sub culture.

Grandin and Atldax portrayed different sides of Cheap Monday, using the skull symbol to arouse curiosity. The designers think that 'the tote bag is the T-shirt of bags: simple, cheap and convenient.'

Karo Akpokiere

The SeekProject

www.seekproject.com

Lagos, Nigeria

If you are raised on 'a robust and consistent diet of cartoons, comic books and drawing time,' you may end up just like Nigerian artist Karo Akpokiere. He knows about being 'that guy who drew a lot in class,' and is a lover of the 'unique and interesting world of urban contemporary visual culture.' He comments that this is 'an art form that is influenced by but not limited to hip-hop culture and all or some of its elements, accessibility, mass- and limited production and individualism.'

This tote bag was a self-initiated project that 'involved using the cost-effective appeal and coolness of the tote bag' to promote his work.

With a powerful personal vibe, the print has a certain tone of independence and creative enthusiasm, qualities imprinted by the artist himself.

Kaza Razat &
Imani Powell

www.spyedesign.com

Harlem, NY, USA

Kaza Razat and Imani Powell run a design studio in New York and are the creative minds behind the Spye brand. Admirers of iconographic design and street art, and former advertising collaborators, they play with an urban-inspired design style.

In a moment between other projects, they imagined something that would allow them to utilize graphic design and that would also be functional – and so this tote design came into life.

This product is full of life, is covered with graphic icons and has an inspiring visual effect.

Where did the inspiration for these icons come from? Kaza and Imani say it was from their childhoods in New York and also from their preference for design icons.

Kazuko Nomoto

www.ba-reps.com

London, UK

Kazuko Nomoto is a London-based illustrator who produces her work under the name Nomoco. Three of Kazuko's designs from 2009 are shown here: 'Growing' shows the city growing, together with the spring; 'Spring' depicts birds about to fly; and 'Drops' features a springtime shower.

The artist's Japanese background may be why these prints are reminiscent of traditional haiku – short poems in a modern graphic version.

An admirer of craftspeople, Kazuko enjoys 'playing with ink and its organic movement.' She finds inspiration in nature and in French horns.

Now we have further proof that art and the eco movement can come together smoothly in products that make our life both greener and more beautiful.

Kittozutto

www.kittozutto.com

Singapore

Kittozutto, the art and design boutique from Singapore 'that believes in the beauty of dreams,' initiated this project without a target audience group in mind, mostly for personal use. The result: a natural product, a white canvas tote with mushroom artwork.

This tote print was one of the boutique's first pieces of illustration work. They considered it a very suitable subject for a tote, as it features a natural theme.

As for the boutique's own work, they describe the style of their creations as modern surrealism. They have many preferred designers and design styles serving as models, but especially those 'with ideas who come up with something fresh.'

Kyle Stewart

Goodhood

www.goodhoodstore.com

London, UK

I never thought that black and white (with occasional spots of red) could be so much fun. Now I have proof that it is possible, from the witty, energetic and well-chosen slogans featured on these Goodhood Store tote bags.

It is often said that an image is worth a thousand words, but these graphic designs from Goodhood make images pale with their own verbal reinforcements.

Combining 'the font Futura, a favourite of 1980s corporate brands and advertising, and messing it up, making it wonky and imperfect with an element of vintage Disney,' Kyle promotes creations with a 'wonky' style to leave the competition behind.

Lucie Sheridan

www.luciesheridan.co.uk

Bristol, UK

After you see the cock, the peacock or the breasts prints made by Lucie Sheridan, you'll probably agree with her own opinion: 'my style has an element of slapstick humour about it.'

Featuring bright colours in a limited palette and simple but bold graphic elements, Lucie's work seems to be created with 'an instinctive lateral, simple approach.' For these print designs, she has explored some words and their literal meaning, without taking them (or herself) too seriously. This is why she thinks anyone can use her bags, even her grandma.

'The tote bag is a great graphic vehicle for communicating with the public,' Lucie believes. She sees totes as 'a natural progression from greetings cards' in her daily printing activity, and also as a bold design item to benefit a world suffocated with plastic bags.

Little Factory

Item Limited

www.littlefactory.com

Hong Kong

Simple and thoughtful design style, simple approach to graphics, simple name: Little Factory. The Hong Kong-based company is actually called Item Limited and they produce subtle graphics for various items.

'Serif Tote Bag' is probably the most minimalist tote you'll ever see. Just looking at the studio's portfolio gives you a pretty good idea about Item Limited's strong passion for letters. Their products give you the advantage of using a highly professional, quality product.

Make Art Your Zoo

www.mayz.jp

Tokyo, Japan

Bright colours, stars, flowers and hearts meet peaceful slogans on the canvases illustrated by MAYZ. That would be 'Make Art Your Zoo' for all of us, and this is how they send a hippy vibe revival all the way from Japan.

We have a whimsical and feminine 'Peace Hand', with lots of stars and an Orient-inspired design all over it, holding a bigger star. There is also the 'Dot Skull', a skull smiling at us with its flowery eyes and decorated with – guess what? – little stars. 'Laura's Heart' is full of flowers and stars. And with the MAYZ logo tote, the list is complete.

Every design is made in a functional, simple, unisex, smart, colourful manner, with the signature style of MAYZ artists Zakee Shariff and Russell Maurice.

Manja Radic

www.njama82.blogspot.com

Belgrade, Serbia

Manja Radic is a Serbian illustrator mainly influenced by working on books for children. 'Positive, funny, melancholic with a bit of child-like naivety' is how she describes her own work.

You can see something of Manja in the self-portrait print, 'The Strong Girl', shown right. It features a tough, strong little girl lifting weights bigger than her while wearing a dress and a pony tail. In the 'Hi Hi Hi Girl' tote design above, the artist was simply playing with the word 'hi'.

Mar Hernández

MalotaProjects

www.malotaprojects.com

Valencia, Spain

With a 'symmetrical, clean, modern and personal' style, Mar Hernández, a.k.a. Malota, designed this tote bag print just for the love of it. No complicated stories about how the idea came up, no aesthetic philosophy behind it, just the love of tote bags.

An illustrator and designer, Mar runs MalotaProjects, a multi-disciplinary studio that develops illustration, design and animation projects. Mar thinks illustrations become much more interesting when they are applied to objects, especially nice, cheap objects such as tote bags.

Mar believes that tote bags have become popular in recent years because they are accessible to a large audience. From the artist's point of view, they represent a very interesting support for developing illustrations and designs.

Marcia Copeland

Swizzlestix

www.swizzlestix.net

San Francisco, USA

'Students, moms, retro buffs, hipsters, and others who love bold and colourful patterns' will probably be interested in these tote bags. Why would they be? Because they can carry 'a variety of things, from library books, small groceries, craft and art supplies, and other everyday items' in a fashionable manner.

Graphic artist Marcia Copeland, from Swizzlestix studio in San Francisco, is a lover of different styles, especially 'eye-catching, fun and vibrant' designs. Therefore, her creations are 'an explosion of colour – bursting with a retro-modern flair, funky and fun, bold and cheerful feel,' in her own description.

Maria Holmer Dahlgren

Metagram

www.metagram.se

Stockholm, Sweden

'A tote bag is not just practical, it's a modern walking billboard. It's a great way to show who you are and what you stand for!' says Maria Holmer Dahlgren from Metagram. She admires Swedish designers from the 1950s, such as Olle Eksell, Stig Lindberg, Sven Markelius, and produces strong, colourful graphic designs like the one shown here.

Modern urban people make the right audience for Maria's design, as eco-consciousness and the popularity of tote bags are already common subjects for them. The artist nowadays has the chance to make themselves heard with the help of totes.

This print design was created in collaboration with Designtorget and LOKA (a Swedish mineral water brand). Maria took inspiration from some of the things that the LOKA brand stands for: 'nature, playfulness, innovation, and the fresh flavour of the mineral water, of course.'

Martynas Birskys

DADADA studio

www.dadadastudio.eu

Vilnius, Lithuania

Based on the philosophy that each image must carry a message, Martynas Birskys from DADADA studio proposes a couple of simple, creative and meaningful prints. No special message written on the totes, nothing to stop your mind wondering what the artist would like to express by that – just white type on black canvas.

Mary Gaynor

www.marygaynor.com

Oakland, CA, USA

Birds, bees and flowers gather together on canvases that are also very practical tote bags for everyone to wear. This Californian graphic artist loves 'the energy and strong visual impact of stencil and freehand art.'

Strong colours and intense imagery influenced by Eastern art make Mary Gaynor's prints come alive and create a positive impact on her audience. She believes in uniqueness, so she uses a combination of printing or stencilling on each bag, with hand-painting, dyeing and/or drawing, so each bag is different. These personal billboards can be used to express humour, political messages or just beauty.

Where does her inspiration come from? She says that themes of nature are important, and using roses, leaves or animal shapes on the bags seems to be instinctive for her.

Mas Shafreen

Wanton Doodle

www.wantondoodle.com

Singapore

'My name is Mas and I am a compulsive doodler.' This is how a confession begins when you ask graphic artist Mas Shafreen to describe himself. He is ready to prove it, with dark circles under his eyes from fervently sketching and scribbling all night.

'Everything's Coming Out Roses' is the name of this tote, produced under the name of the Wanton Doodle company. The creator reveals its meaning: 'the gravity of any situation is very dependent on perception, so anything can be beautiful, even projectile discharge.'

Megan Price

Mr.PS

www.mr-ps.co.uk

Greater Manchester, UK

Who doesn't like to have a choice, whether it concerns fashion or ecology? For those of us who reserve the right to change our minds, Megan Price has created the '(In)Decision' bag. Inspired by the graphics of everyday life, she promotes a bold, simple, effective style, for 'teenagers to sixty-somethings.'

This tote was created to meet the need for a 'stylish reusable bag to take to the local farmers' market and baker's on a Saturday morning,' says Megan. Hand-screenprinted with 'Yes please' on one side and 'No thanks' on the other, its message will come across one way or another.

Some things are certain though: this tote bag is 'perfect for carrying bottles of wine, library books, some knitting and who knows what else. It can also be rolled up into a handbag ready for use in case of any impulse shopping.'

Medicom

www.medicomtoystore.com

Tokyo, Japan

This fabulous tote bag is the result of a collaboration between Medicom Fabrick and English artist Will Sweeney's Alakazam label. The all-over print featuring a monster-inspired theme is a signature work from Sweeney, who teamed up with the textile side of Medicom on a series of items including this tote bag.

With a style that quickly wins enthusiastic followers, the creation signed by Will Sweeney is very likely to create a cult.

The fabric of the tote is described by its creators as: 'guaranteed to be stimulating to mind and body,' and 'to provide visual excitement within everyday life.'

Mel Lim

www.mellim.com

San Diego, CA, USA

'We all want a tote today, especially totes that are fun, fashionable and functional without putting a hole in the wallet,' says designer Mel Lim. An admirer of edgy designers such as Alexander McQueen, she describes her own style in three words: 'joy, luxe and modern.' Her ideas are best illustrated in the Joy collection, a modern approach to nature featuring flowers, animals and landscapes.

The idea of producing totes was in fact a fan's request. Mel responded to the request, and created some cool totes in different sets of fresh colour schemes. So everybody got what they wanted: moms, kids, designers, architects, students, and anyone interested in being stylish and making a green statement at the same time. No more monochrome, mundane tote prints: Mel Lim brings fun and joy to tote designs.

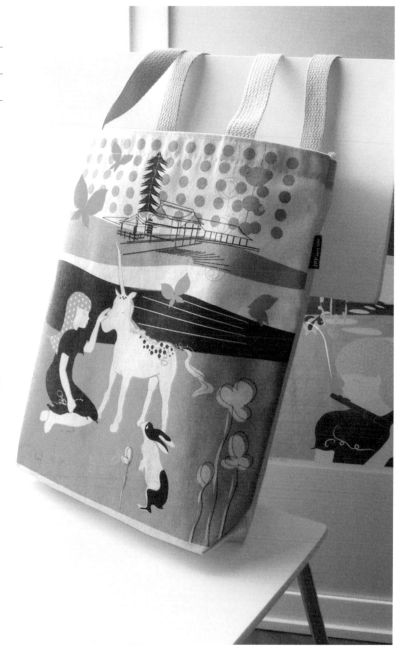

Miguel Melgarejo

Miguel Melgarejo Design

www.migmel.com

Monterrey, Mexico

We've probably all heard about the global village, but what about the Urban Farm? This is a set of supermarket shopping tote bags, aimed to 'capture attention, encourage reflection and create change,' from designer Miguel Melgarejo.

Miguel Melgarejo is an industrial designer who likes to create metaphor-based products. One of his goals is to generate value through design, so he concentrates on 'objects that are based on exploiting elements of human behaviour.' The tote was chosen as an object that conveys simple, environmentally conscious messages that have an impact on the community's behaviour.

Morris Lee

Momorobo

www.momorobo.com

Singapore and Shanghai, China

The world of tote bags has become vast lately and offers a wealth of choices. Maybe, as a tote bag fan, you sometimes fancy something 'versa-style'? Here you have a sample from someone who fancies the concept itself, Morris Lee, a digital freelancer at Wieden + Kennedy Shanghai and also at Momorobo, a visual lab from Singapore producing illustration and graphic design.

Inspired by the traditional Oriental technique of woodblock printing, this tote bag print was made by Momorobo for a competition curated by Wieden + Kennedy Shanghai.

The tote bag features some familiar Momorobo characters; feisty robot-like creatures, on a crowded urban background, between buildings and black clouds, appear on both sides of the bag.

Tote bags may be considered a cheap and popular choice for the masses at present, but they also provide a large canvas for artwork – a compelling reason why graphic artists use them in their attempt to appeal to a mass audience.

Nadja Girod

Smil

www.smil.biz

Berlin, Germany

Looking for something colourful to cheer up your day? How about 'Von Berlin in die Welt' – a cute girl on a bike who seems ready to travel all the way from Berlin to the world? Or the 'Ahoi' bag, with an apparently shy sailor cat greeting us?

These 'simple, happy' designs come from a screenprinting studio in Berlin. German illustrator Nadja Girod designed these prints for people 'who like simple colourful designs.' The 'Ahoi' bag was the first tote she created, with the message, 'summer full speed ahead.' The other, translated as 'From Berlin', was designed for 'all those world travellers who start in Berlin.' It can also be seen as a good souvenir 'for non-tourists who are proud to be Berliner and want to show the world.'

Nadja strives 'for a design aesthetic that is somewhere between skulls and butterflies, neither too cute, nor too cool.' Also, as a fashion design student and apprentice pattern-drafter, Nadja has a passion for creating patterns for textiles.

Nina Palmer

Platform Design

www.platformdesign.ca

Vancouver, Canada

People who like to cook, chefs and anyone who wants a good sturdy bag, here's good news for you! Nina Palmer has created the 'Kitchen' tote bag, inspired by the contents of her own kitchen and its utensils.

Illustrator Nina enjoys art and design that plays off everyday things and spaces in a particular organic, detailed style. For this design, she wanted to get more of a human touch, so she hand-drew on the actual bag, photographed it and then used special software to finalize the design.

Noëla Parant

www.noelaparant.com

London, UK

'It's important to be as green as we can, but it can also be fun,' is the credo of Noëla Parant regarding totes. A French designer, living and working in London, Noëla loves to draw and finds the tote bag a nice object to work on.

She works freestyle, doing whatever she imagines and letting it change every day. Therefore, inspiration can come from everywhere. In a complicated and baroque-like style with a minimalistic choice of colours,

Noëla's prints look striking on white canvases. This print is a personal representation of the heart symbol, set amid floral and vegetable motifs.

Artistic skills take over modern ways of expression, making the tote bag 'a space to put ideas and beautiful designs.' Wearing a tote comes mostly from ecological motives, but there is fashion inspiration there too; 'you can choose your tote bag of the day, just like you choose your tee or shoes,' concludes Noëla.

Paul Farrell

www.paul-farrell.co.uk

Kent, UK

Strong contrasts of colours and graphic effects, with an interesting combination of shapes and silhouettes: these are the elements that make up Paul Farrell's graphic art style.

These totes, with their simple combinations of singular symbols on mono-coloured backgrounds, make a refreshing sight for the eyes.

Pepa Prieto

www.pepaprieto.com

Granada, Spain

Brightly coloured and oozing joy and amazement, Pepa Prieto's designs make any object come to life through the strong infusion of her imagination.

Pepa creates stunning artwork, and from first sight of these tote prints you can see that she loves colours and wonderful adventures. Fantastic human-like characters, accompanied by birds, travel through space and time, as in the 'Present Past Future' tote shown right.

The idea of motion and travelling is present in her other designs, too – either a bird or a bicycle helps the main characters to get on their way, while rain or petals fall all over the place.

The artist thinks that the tote bag is 'a great item to make an intervention,' a reason to decorate something that is useful, 'light and resistant' at the same time.

Pianofuzz

www.pianofuzz.com

Londrina, Brazil

Have you ever heard the song 'The Three Mushrooms', by the Brazilian singer Gilberto Gil? If you haven't, you might try to visualize it from the design of Pianofuzz design studio, who took inspiration from its lyrics.

Edmarlon Semprebom, owner and designer of Pianofuzz, encourages experimentation and collective production. Pianofuzz 'realizes and creates in a free way, always looking to overcome expectations, for visual refinement and the materialization of concepts.'

Funny, colourful and intriguing, the design studio's tote bags suit anyone concerned about environmental and global issues and who wants to carry around something original.

Proud Creative

www.proudcreative.com

London, UK

Proud is a multi-disciplinary design studio that aims 'to create work that makes our clients and everyone at the studio proud.' They designed these tote bags as promotional items for two of their clients. The 'Glo London' tote, shown above, was used as a promotional device to retain the attention of art buyers. The 'Getty Images HOW' tote, shown right, was created to drive new registrants to the Getty Images website. Both bags were produced by Progress Packaging (see p. 122).

Designer James Greenfield from Proud Creative sees the tote bag as 'an easy slogan device where people can broadcast a message or style.'

Progress Packaging

www.progresspkg.co.uk

Huddersfield, UK

Progress Packaging collaborated with a variety of design studios including The Designers Republic, SEA, Spin, Airside and NB:Studio to produce these totes. The bags were designed for Re-Bag, an exhibition of limited-edition canvas bags curated by Progress Packaging.

The brief was to create an image for a bag with a theme of sustainability and reusability. All the bags were screenprinted white on a Pantone-matched grey canvas. The designs were kept as simple as possible, with just one colour. 'This way the message of the design would be kept functional and simple,' comments Simon Farrow, a graphic artist from Progress Packaging.

The ideal target audience for these bags are people who want to signal their environmental standpoint, as well as their tastes and desires, through good design.

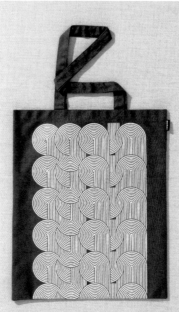

This page, clockwise from top left:

Multistorey

Supermundane

NB:Studio (two images)

Airside

Opposite page, clockwise from top left:

BB Saunders

Browns

Non Format

Saturday

Design Project (two images)

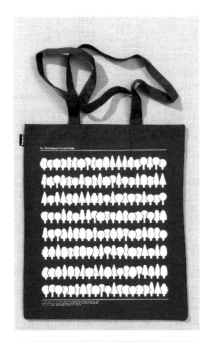

Rachel Gannon

INK Illustration

www.inkillustration.com

London, UK

The illustrations of Rachel Gannon from INK Illustration look as if they have landed directly from her personal sketchbooks and journals. Doodles, drawings and notes scribbled on the white canvas of a reusable tote bag make her prints instantly recognizable and help the designs stand out in a crowd.

As well as being inspired by sketchbooks, Rachel says she depicts 'the feral cats that haunt our studio.'

Rachel Rheingold
&
Michael Berick

Maptote

www.maptote.com

Brooklyn, NY, USA

A tote bag that is also a city map – who could ask for more? Flashing a style that is 'tongue and cheek with a bit of nostalgia,' you can walk the streets carelessly: there's no way you can get lost with a tote like this on your shoulder.

Rachel Rheingold and Michael Berick, the brains behind Maptote, were initially inspired by European totes that drew upon city landmarks. They target the bags at a specific audience consisting of the 'environmentally conscious, and fashionistas.'

Rob Marshbank

www.marshbank.net

Philadelphia, PA, USA

Graphic designer and illustrator Rob Marshbank designed this lumberjack tote for clients of advertising agency Red Tettemer. Its purpose was to be given as a holiday gift, along with a matching card with the message, 'Wishing you a very fuzzy holiday.'

Rob describes his style of work as 'sometimes quirky, illustration-based design,' and he says he loves the cartoon styles of the 1960s and 70s. Fittingly enough, this tote bag displays a humorous image to fit its humorous message, guaranteed to make you smile.

Ros Shiers

Ros Shiers (I heart RS)

www.ros-shiers.com

London, UK

Matryoshka dolls combined with complex patterns and Japanese optical icons; 'Love' and 'Hate' prints on each side of a bag; burlesque femmes fatales with a love of nature all come together in Ros Shiers' world, in beautifully intricate detail. She combines a love of pattern and detail with strong, bold, graphic illustration.

The London-based label, I heart RS, run by designer Ros, produces a boutique range of tote prints. Unique illustrations are screenprinted in black on 100 per cent organic cotton, combining the practical with the beautiful.

People of all ages, styles and tastes may find these prints enjoyable, as they are inspired by childhood memories and stories such as *Alice in Wonderland*. They give you a good reason to wear something eco-friendly.

Russell Reid

Wasted Heroes

www.wastedheroes.com

Liverpool, UK

When you enjoy screenprinting and experimenting with colours and shapes, tote bags can prove to be as attractive as T-shirts. Russell Reid, founder of the UK indie T-shirt label Wasted Heroes, can confirm this.

In a bold and bright style that can be slightly twisted, he creates designs such as 'Droplet Face', 'J'aime la discothèque' and 'Swirling Face' – colourful, visually appealing and very graphic.

Designing and screenprinting on his own, Russell Reid embraced inspiration for these prints from a mixture of 1980s album covers, Pop Art and 'I heart NY' T-shirts and bags.

Rupert Meats

Rude

www.thisisrude.com

London, UK

Despite the name of Rupert Meats' company, there's nothing 'rude' about carrying your favourite tote, especially if you want to make a personal and an eco statement. Pretty much everyone can react positively to these boldly coloured modern design proposals.

Graphic artist Rupert admires painters such as David Hockney, but he uses a more modern style to create his own designs.

Rupert sells a lot of screenprints, so he thought it made sense to put them onto other products. He likes the tote bag because it provides a great medium for print and graphic image-making, and he believes the tote bag is now a serious rival to the T-shirt. We don't really see people giving up their T-shirts yet, but we see more and more people using tote bags, 'because no one should be using plastic bags any more!' as Rupert declares.

Sara Hoover

Small Screen Designs

www.smallscreendesigns.com

Cleveland, OH, USA

Iconic objects of the post-consumerist era, such as the shopping cart, along with ecological symbols, such as the bicycle, find their place in Sara Hoover's simple, graphic tote prints. 'Each of my designs merges the familiar with the creative, transforming life into art,' says Sara.

Sara's company, Small Screen Designs, produces these interesting items, especially targeting eco shoppers. Sara's motivation in creating these prints was to expose the beauty that is all around us, as well as responding to the 'go green' movement and wishing to eliminate extra waste.

Sara likes screenprinted poster art, and is influenced by the works of 1960s Pop artist Andy Warhol. The artist believes in the 'simple use of line art to encourage people to look at everyday objects in a new way,' bringing a different perspective to everyday objects that are so often taken for granted.

Sara Jensen

Lost Bird Found

www.lostbirdfound.com

Pacific Northwest, USA

Illustrator Sara Jensen from Lost Bird Found studio uses her imagination to create designs for various tastes. The style that results is organic and accessible, and usually hand-drawn. Black and white designs feature, but also playful coloured ones, inspired by heraldry, medieval illustration, and family crests.

Sara Jensen understands the pleasure of owning beautiful bags. Combining this with her love of drawing, especially of food and animals, tote bags seemed like a natural outlet for this artist.

The 'Pomegranate', 'Damask' and 'Bird' totes shown here are meant to appeal to everybody, both in design and in function; unpretentious designs that are also indisputably useful.

Sarah J. Coleman

Inkymole

www.inkymole.com

Midlands, UK

Illustrator Sarah J. Coleman of Inkymole creates 'hands-on, ink-heavy, often word-soaked imagery.' Among her preferred artists are people who can capture a huge amount of drama and tell stories. Add to Sarah's passion for drawing the need to share an ecological message, and the results are these inspiring tote designs.

Sarah's inspiration came from simply looking at the landscape and realizing that birds are some of the species that suffer most from our chaotic treatment of the environment. Sarah wanted these prints to touch a wide audience – men and women, parents, teenagers and anyone who cares for nature's beauties.

Sky high
hopes
hatching
hungry and green

Sarah Wilkins

www.sarahwilkins.net

Paris, France

If you wonder why this tote design is reminiscent of a children's book illustration, it is because author Sarah Wilkins is better known for illustrating books and magazines than designing bags. This particular design was made for bookseller Barnes and Noble, with women who love to read in mind.

The clarity, simplicity and beauty that Sarah herself admires are also found in her 'Afternoon Stroll' tote bag, with its clear, soft colours, uncomplicated story and cursive shapes.

Sarah is based in Paris, France, another reason why she describes her own work as 'poetic, delicate, feminine, graceful and whimsical.'

Sarajo Frieden

www.sarajofrieden.com

Los Angeles, CA, USA

The tree is a symbol that is frequently used to represent ecological issues. In this tote print, graphic artist Sarajo Frieden gives the tree image a more personal twist and also a musical association. The image, 'Violin Tree', was originally created as a painting. It is based on the idea that trees are the 'lungs of the planet,' says Sarajo, as well as being symbols of 'solidity and rootedness'.

Commissioned by the company Poketo, this design was meant to act as an antidote to horrifying environmental scenarios such as the 'giant garbage patch floating in the north Pacific' or 'becoming buried in plastic bags.'

Sarajo declares 'nature, music, folk tales, puppets, Paul Klee, textiles, Hungarian grandparents and the films of Jacques Tati' among her sources of inspiration. She doesn't define her style in a specific manner, but only as an 'evolving style'.

Shinzi Katoh

Shinzi Katoh Design

www.shinzikatoh.com

Kasugai City, Japan

Japanese designer Shinzi Katoh's collection of totes focuses on cute, naive elements from childhood and stories, such as those dedicated to the adorable Little Red Riding Hood, or characters such as pet friends.

The designer tries to imbue his style with peacefulness. His motivation for designing tote prints is to create something funny and new that makes people happy. For this noble purpose, inspiration can come from almost everywhere, including travel, whether within Japan or to other countries.

And if these totes somehow fail to make people happy, at least they benefit the environment.

Sonia Brit

Bob Boutique

www.bob.net.au

Victoria, Australia

'Beautiful illustrations that are innocent and take you to another world in a glance' are Sonia Brit's speciality. She favours designs from pre-1980s children's story books, and her inspiration comes from childhood memories such as 'the games we used to play, the books we used to read and the words we used to use.'

Sonia's designs, on offer at Bob Boutique, are 'eye-catchingly cute'. So if you like practical items with a load of emotional energy, you could use Sonia's 'sweet happy prints' every day.

Stefan Tijs

www.stefantijs.com

Rotterdam, The Netherlands

The inspiration for this delightful tote came from the song 'Happy When It Rains'; Dutch designer Stefan Tijs decided to take the song title and make an image for it.

If Stefan could describe his style of work – which he doesn't like to, because 'anything he might say feels limiting,' it would probably be 'clean, bold and colourful.'

Stewart Walker

www.zeropoint25.com

Glasgow, UK

If typography could come to life, it would probably choose to do so in one of Stewart Walker's designs. These prints were created 'to be sold in a fictional typography museum shop.'

Stewart wanted to 'celebrate the diversity of typeface design by exploiting each letter's individual character.' This is why the type plays all around the canvases. 'On one side, the type sits harmoniously together; on the reverse, gravity has taken over and forced the letters to the bottom of the bag, bringing the type to life,' he explains.

Stewart likes lean, modernist design, but finds inspiration in all walks of life. His philosophy and style of work is 'simple and conceptually sound'. He embraces all aspects of design in order to grow and progress.

Suzie Brown

Urban Bird Design & Illustration

www.urbanbird.co.uk

Hampshire, UK

Urban Bird products aim to draw attention to nature in urban environments and the landscape: 'birds, plants and trees cohabit in urban surroundings despite competition for space from the needs and plans of man and the built environment, and can offer mystery and other-worldliness,' explains designer Suzie Brown.

The results are seen in these beautiful totes – colourful, contemporary and evocative in style. Suzie comments that 'there is a need for more interesting designs and colours', to liven up the use of tote bags.

Suzie says she is influenced by Japanese kimono fabrics and prints, among other things.

listen globally play locally **expansion team**

Tatiana Arocha

www.tatianaarocha.com

Brooklyn, NY, USA

New York-based designer Tatiana Arocha is among those who choose to express environmental messages with the help of tote canvas. This 'Expansion Team' tote bag was inspired by rainforests.

The designer targets a wide audience, but especially those who would enjoy wearing tote bags with nature-related themes in order to protect the environment.

Tofu Girls

www.tofugirls.com

Temple City, CA, USA

Created 'by women for women', the Tofu Girls' collection of totes makes a colourful and lively statement about the power of imagination and creativity. Pirates, evil stars, skulls and spooky characters inspired by Japanese comics live in a world that could be really scary if depicted differently. But the playful darker tones usually remain in the cute anime (Japanese animation) area, giving the designs a feminine vibe more than a gothic one.

Made on sturdy canvas, printed with various creatures, always in motion, in well-chosen vibrant colours, the totes promoted by Tofu Girls are an obvious choice for modern style fans.

Tommy Higson

www.tommyeugenehigson.
blogspot.com

Oldham, UK

Some images are so firmly lodged in our collective consciousness that we don't really notice them any more. Tommy Higson is a designer who likes to restore those images by making something new and cool out of them.

As today's 'new and cool' involves wearing a tote bag, Tommy thinks 'you can get a handy cheap bag that feels really personal to you.' An admirer of 'contemporary illustration and so-called lowbrow art,' Tommy tries to keep his designs fun and accessible. He describes his style as 'post-Pop fashion illustration,' but with a vast subject range.

Tommy says he tries to offer people 'images that are elegant and perhaps a bit delicate.'

Toormix

www.toormix.com

Barcelona, Spain

Creative + visual + humour + colour. This is the equation used by the Toormix studio to reveal their message. Creating an appealing bag is not always easy, especially when the market is full of 'easy, cheap and creative' stuff – beautiful creations by talented artists.

The artists from Barcelona who created these totes speak loudly in a minimal and conceptual style, with a smart use of colours and shapes. The 'Day & Night' bag has two sides, one for going shopping (the 'Day'/orange side) and the other side for going out (the 'Night'/white side). The 'I'm Out of the Office' bag plays with the idea of leisure, using the phrase people typically leave on their automated email and telephone messages when they're away from their desks.

Ulla Puggaard

www.ullapuggaard.com

London, UK

Ulla Puggaard is an illustrator and art director with a background in graphic design, illustration and art. Her name is Danish, her inspiration comes from the Scandinavian way of life, but her work is done in London.

Inspired by anyone who creates striking work, she claims that 'Scandinavians tend not to draw distinctions between creative disciplines.' Ulla keeps herself open to a wide variety of influences, including textile design, architecture and sculpture, Mother Nature, modern-day artists and architects, and Pablo Picasso.

A passion for striking forms, strong colours and functionality is visible in her bold, graphic style. Ulla designed these tote bags when she was working on quotes for a magazine, and liked them enough to print them and display them proudly.

She regards the tote bag as a moving canvas; 'affordable, fashionable, personal items' that are suitable for anyone.

Valerie Thai

Cabin + Cub Design

www.cabinandcub.com

Vancouver, Canada

Canadian illustrator Valerie Thai's works are 'simple, modern and fun, with a child-like quality.' Much of the work output by Valerie's company, Cabin + Cub Design, is graphic and bold, as reflected in this cheery tote featuring a bright orange bird design.

The bag was designed in response to Valerie's personal need for eco-friendly grocery bags: 'I was tired of all the plastic and paper bags that we were using when we went to the market,' she explains.

Valerie also mentions being 'eco chic' and making stylistic choices as reasons why many individuals carry their goods around in an eco-conscious tote bag.

From this artist's point of view, the tote is also the perfect blank canvas on which to create her designs.

Valistika Studio

www.valistika.com

Barcelona, Spain

When graphics meet typography, interesting designs come out, mixing handmade and digital drawing, collage and painting. What else is to be expected from a creative Spanish couple like Guadalupe Cos-Gayon Alía and Miguel Abio Ruiz from Valistika Studio?

This print was inspired by the pair's personal experience of moving to Barcelona, a goal that took a lot of effort and which shows in the struggling design of the tote. Friendly and scary, optimistic and anxious, crowded and contrasting, this is an image of inner and outer battles, and yet is a 'comfortable and easy-to-wear product for young people.'

Vicky Newman

Fine and Dandy Illustrations

www.vickynewman.com

London, UK

Vicky Newman is a freelance illustrator who works with a blend of hand-drawn line and digital colour. For those looking for a combination of art history and old-school aesthetics, Vicky's designs are the perfect choice.

The tote prints shown here come from Vicky's 'Wits and Dandies' series. The designs combine the tote bag – a modern mode of expression – with images of 'whiskered gentlemen in elaborate suits' together with quotes from Oscar Wilde, the ultimate wit and dandy.

Vicky's influences include Aubrey Beardsley and Art Nouveau, with 'a little bit of nonsense thrown in for good measure.' This artist also loves the Victoriana look and 2B propelling pencils (8B for shadows).

Her motivation for creating the prints was creating a reusable canvas tote bag to use instead of plastic bags.

Yi Yu Shen

Studio in Blooom

www.inblooom.com

Taiwan

Taiwanese artist Yi Yu Shen's designs feature simple, soft, delicate elements, and quiet, graceful colour combinations. His prints, created with a team under the name of Studio in Blooom, avoid strong elements and try to express emotions gradually.

Yi Yu believes in creations that are good at telling stories and that can touch the heart. His patterns are inspired by his homeland – Taiwanese native animals and traditional interior decorations, for instance.

'I hope my designs can call forth people's consideration for our environment and animals,' says the artist. One of his totes features an endangered species of native bird, the Crested Myna, which has been threatened by the invasion of non-native species. The tote bag bears witness to the bird's plight in a delicate and poignant way.

Zaihasriah Zahidi

Dotiro

zaihasriah.wordpress.com

Kuala Lumpur, Malaysia

Zaihasriah Zahidi of Dotiro studio declares, 'We adore design that has a sense of doodle-ish, whimsical fun with colourful elements.' Dotiro have a colourful, surreal style in which lots of unexpected objects appear out of nowhere, combining pure and imaginative illustrations with a naive feeling. They say that 'experimenting with things and just following what our mind is telling us to draw' is one of their main principles.

Dotiro believes that tote bags are a great medium for transferring imaginative illustrations onto canvas. They also like to make art that is wearable – and totes are both wearable and very convenient, as 'you can put whatever you like in one whole bag.' Wearing something attractive that is also intriguing is one of the modern consumer's main goals when looking for the right tote.

Zeke Wade

Doje

www.doje.co.uk

London, UK

With inspiration coming from so many sources, ranging from 'heraldic shields to geometric design to Victorian illustration and typography,' how could you ever get bored of your tote bag?

London-based illustrator Zeke Wade extracts interesting subjects from various sources, and draws his designs in a pen-and-ink-based style. With unexpected themes and details, we may conclude that his goal of 'drawing the viewer into the image through intricate design and thought-provoking elements' is being reached with these designs.

Zena McKeown &
Ben Roberts

Me & Zena

www.meandzena.com

London, UK

If you have looked in vain for romantic-themed designs, search no more. Me & Zena, the London studio that is the brainchild of designer Zena McKeown, will satisfy your love of all things small, shiny and symbolic.

Thousands of 'unruly girls' across the world now have the chance to share Zena's appetite for cute things like 'unicorns, gold and love.'

What about the design that states our right to remain romantic? This tote was designed to get the Me & Zena brand message out into the world with a bold graphic statement. Zena and Ben Roberts designed this graphic bag, inspired by the 1979 song 'Romantic Rights' by Death From Above. Zena says, 'I just loved the idea that romance is a basic human right, and being a wordy person I couldn't resist the alliteration!'

Zeptonn

www.zeptonn.nl

Groningen, The Netherlands

It isn't always necessary to be schooled in art, especially when talent and imagination are involved – self-taught designer Jan Willem Wennekes is living proof of that. He also demonstrates that artistic inclinations co-exist successfully with scientific passion (he studied Artificial Intelligence and Philosophy at the University of Groningen).

Jan now works as an illustrative designer and art director under the name Zeptonn, in Studio Pats, a collective studio in the Netherlands.

Zeptonn's world is populated by critters and monsters, sharing bold colours, a world of oppositions, street art, fair trade, eco-friendliness, music and philosophy. Jan illustrates sketchbooks, T-shirts, skateboards, posters, wall decals, bags, wallets, books and more. This tote design, 'Follow Your Dream', shows off his fantasy-rich style.

Zosen

Animal Bandido

www.animalbandido.com

Barcelona, Spain

Zosen Font admires 'people doing good stuff with the do-it-yourself spirit.' He turns a 'shamanic enthusiasm' into ritual, folklore and symbolism to develop his own iconography and art practice that critiques the current social and political climate.

'Relationships, life, death, ecology, bad trips, carnival, animals, circuses' – you may not see the logical thread between these, but that's okay – this is just the whimsical world where Zosen's inspiration comes from. He thinks that his work 'builds a playful narrative with abstract characters and symbols that dance across cityscapes, boldly breaking rules and expanding the dialogue with the city.'

For Zosen, tote bags are the nearest approach to public art that an artist can afford in Barcelona. They also represent a sign of changing attitudes with regard to ecological issues.

Thanks

I would like to thank the people who answered the call for entries for the book. I am grateful for the high standard of submissions I received; the work I received for the book surpassed my greatest expectations.

I would like to thank my publisher, Laurence King, and his team who provided me with guidance while compiling this book: Helen Rochester, Clare Double and Angus Hyland.

I would like to give my appreciation to those generous people who spared time from their busy schedules and forwarded me to other potential contributors. My special thanks go to these individuals who gave me guidance and inspired me: Mark Champkins, Gavin o'Carol, Alex Hammond, Martin Vowels, Vishal Shah, Sarah J. Coleman, Central Illustration Agency, Bernstein and Andriulli, Russell Maurice, Angus Hyland, Zeptonn, Christopher and Kathleen Sleboda, Kyle Stewart, eBoy, Paul Farrell, Andrew Bannecker, Ulla Puggaard, Jon Burgerman, Ben Smith, Elena Luján Gonzalo and Ana Rico Robles.

I would also like to thank my clients and the fans of my work who have been a positive energy in my life and career, especially my family, my parents, Dinkerrai and Parvatiben, and my friends for being supportive.

Additional credits:

p12 Bags produced and sold by Envelop, www.envelop.eu
p14 Bags produced by The Outfit
pp18–19 Designer Fabian Herrmann
p21 Bag made by Ian Dunlop
p22 Photography by Peter van Dijk, www.petervandijk.net. Thanks to envelop.eu
p27 Design and printing Carla Rosado and Hugo Henriques
p28 © copyright Champ and Rosie
p29 www.catalinaestrada.com / www.panchotolchinsky.com
p30 Peter Blake for the Royal Parks Foundation
p31 Agency: Thinkhouse PR, Client: Ben & Jerry's
p33 It's OK bag: Anthony Burrill
p35 Jim Datz, www.neitherfishnorfowl.com
p40 Cut-Out, www.cutoutshop.com. Bags screenprinted by Kay Stanley
p44 Photography Cesar Segarra, make-up Raquel Galván, art direction Elena Gallen and Dracula Studio, styling Raquel Galván and Elena Gallen
p46 Client: Five Leaves Inc., Japan
p49 Gabrijela Bulatovic, Dunja Savic
p50 www.socialdesigner.com
p53 MHG Design
p57 All © copyright Chip Chop Designs, 2006–2010
p60 'Suicide Kings' (bottom) created for Compound Gallery
p61 Photography Nathan Beddows
p63 'Buy me a Drink' Joe Stewart, 'Gold, Weed, Money' Clayton Crocker, 'I'm a Designer' design Badrul Rupak, copywriting Joe Stewart
p65 Screenprinted by Darling Clementine and Graham Hayward
p67 © copyright Jason Scuderi/Antimotion
p71 © copyright Joe Rogers
p72 Client: The Outfit, agent: Bernstein and Andriulli
p75 www.burgerplex.com
p79 Bag produced by The Outfit
p80 Photography: pink and grey bags by Julia Nielsen, yellow and black bags by Scandinavianwave.se
p81 Screenprinting: Supreme Creations
p90 Photography Taye Idahor, printing www.cutoutshop.com
p91 © copyright Spye Design Studio, LLC
p91 Bags produced by The Outfit
p93 Printed on Bdiff tote bags
p95 Kyle Stewart/Jo Swdle
p98 Design ChiFun Wong
p102 © copyright Swizzlestix
p111 Designed with Cristina Gutiérrez, photography by Verónica Valdés Vega
p112–113 Medicom Toy Life Entertainment™ and © 2005–2010 Medicom Toy Corporation. All rights reserved. © Will Sweeney
p115 © copyright BYOB, bringyourownbag.ca
p116 With thanks to Envelop.eu
p117 Printer: Printed Textiles, Swindon
p120 Pianofuzz Design Studio for Poketo
p121 © copyright Proud Creative
p122 Exhibition and print design by Design Project
p127 Photography Kate Mathis
p128 Julia Cagninelli
p132 Abi Williams
p137 'Sky High Hopes' for Howard Chang at The Outfit, produced by The Outfit. Agent Bernstein and Andriulli, New York
p143 © copyright 2009 Stefan Tijs
p146 Design by Çamila Arocha, Lojja Designs
p147 Hong Ly, founder
p151 Photography Roger Allen
p152 © copyright Valistika Studio
p154 Chiu, Chung-Yu and Tsai, Wen-Hui
p155 Jazmi Izwan Jamal